D1487053

New York 16, N.Y.

THERE'S A FUTURE FOR TEACHERS

There's a Future For Teachers

A Practical Classroom Guide

N. Estella Finley

EXPOSITION PRESS · NEW YORK

FIRST EDITION

I Chose Teaching

"and they'll sit before you
with bright, eager faces."

But now you know that sometimes
Their faces
Aren't so eager,
Aren't so bright.
Often they are
Dirty, hungry, poor, questioning,
Openly antagonistic.

"But I will try," you say—

Trying *isn't* enough today.
You must *Do!*
These children need you.
The country needs you.
The quality of its future depends on you.

—Marilyn O. Evans
Class of 1935
Chicago Teachers College

PREFACE

It seems a long time since I gave up teaching in 1947. After my parents passed away, teaching was my greatest interest in life. I still retain my interest in the work of my teacher friends and youth. Many of my former students confide in me yet concerning their plans, college careers and romances. Some have an idea of becoming teachers. This gave me the idea that I might be of service to them and others of their kind. So I am writing some suggestions for the beginning teachers.

I am not assuming that my suggestions are the only way or even the best way of doing things. However, I have had some measure of success in using them. With my sincere desire to be helpful, I have kept away from any conventional style of writing. These years of teaching have convinced me that the youth of today are less conventional than when I was a beginning teacher.

Almost a year has passed since I completed the book. I find myself just now putting the finishing touches on the work. Only the persevering encouragement of my friends gave me the courage to bring this book before the public.

Now I leave *There's a Future for Teachers* up to the readers, hoping that their contemplation will bring me an expression of approval.

N. Estella Finley

Michigan City, Indiana

CONTENTS

INTRODUCTION

So They Say

"If America is to be run by the people, it is the people who must think. And we do not need to put on sackcloth and ashes to think. Nor should our minds work like a sundial, which records only sunshine. Our thinking must square against some lessons of history, some principles of government and morals, if we would preserve the rights and dignity of men to which this nation is dedicated."

—Ex-President Herbert Hoover

The Happiest Way

BY EDGAR A. GUEST*

There is so much to know, so little time to learn;
So many corners on life's road, one wonders which to turn;
This one may lead to pleasure gay, and this to wisdom true,
And this, if we would follow it, might lead to friendships new;
Yet none can ever tread them all, nor drain life's cup of bliss—
Chance leads us to the joys we find and past the joys we miss.

We know that some paths lead to shame, and some to grief
    and woe;
But there are byways, here and there, whose ends we'll
    never know.
And there are roads we'd like to tread, yet duty spurs us on,
And there are goals we'd like to reach, yet we must strive for one.
Not all of life is ours to know, not all its work we do;
The race of men to come shall learn some truths we never knew.

At best we blindly rush along; in haste we love or spurn,
And what we miss another claims, and misses in his turn.
There is so much for man to know, so little time to choose;
For every joy we win from life, we pay with joys we lose.
No one of mortal clay has solved the secret of life's plan.
The happiest way is for us all to do the best we can.

THERE'S A FUTURE FOR TEACHERS

SHIRLEY'S IDEAL TEACHER

The girls had gone to the beach to get cool. The forenoon had been one of those hot June days that the Midwest experiences. They were summer students at the university center in their home town, located at the southern tip of Lake Michigan. Each had plans to go to the campus the following winter. They had done some cadet teaching the last semester of their high school work. They had a notion to prepare to be teachers. Naturally their conversation turned towards their recent school days, since they had just finished high school. Betty, a tall blonde of seventeen years, cast aside the top of her blue sun-suit, which reflected the blue of her eyes as she sat on the sand. She said in doleful tones, "Oh, if I could ever be a good teacher, I'd be glad to try it. . . . Some of those children in the classes with which I helped this last semester were darlings."

"Of course you can be a good teacher if you just go on being the kind of person you are now," replied Shirley, the dark, chubby girl, as she lounged upon the sand beside Betty. The girls had been close friends ever since Shirley had come to the city during their freshman year. In fact, Betty had rescued Shirley from her state of bewilderment at that time. Being a timid person, Shirley found it difficult to make friends. She was very unhappy in her first days at school.

"Whatever do you mean?" inquired Betty.

"I mean just what I said, goofy," replied Shirley. Her black eyes sparkled as she added with a laugh, "You are much like my favorite teacher, whom I shall never forget."

"Me!—like your favorite teacher!" exclaimed Betty.

"That's a joke!" replied Shirley. Soberly she continued, "When I was to enter the sixth grade I was forced to change schools. Our family moved more than anybody I ever knew. This time we moved to a rural home and I had to go to a one-room school. Everything was strange to me, as I had never lived in the country. It was harder for me than when I came here and you came to my rescue."

"I guess you dreaded going to school the first day," interrupted Betty.

"It was not the thought of starting school, but getting acquainted with the new pupils, teacher and other things. I always loved school," confided Shirley.

"Knowing you as I do, you need not tell me that," assented Betty.

Continuing, Shirley said, "The school was a one-room affair the like of which you have never seen. There are so few in our state. This was out West. There were many new things for me to get acquainted with besides the people. The teacher was little older than some of the pupils. She was a short blonde lady and seemed not more grown-up than some of the big girls. But she had a sweet dignity that I, though just a child, noticed. She won me at once. She never raised her voice. It was soft and musical. Some of the big girls had loud, harsh tones. Her speech was rapid and lively. The recitations of the older ones seemed like pleasant conversations to me. Our recess periods were made enjoyable by her participation in our games. I was soon at ease in my class. My teacher was a new friend and playmate."

"Did she have such a good education?" interrupted Betty.

"Little did I think of that. But as I remember, she was able to answer questions, or we all looked up the answers," Shirley recalled.

"She must have been qualified to teach or she would not

have had a position. How foolish of me to ask that!" returned Betty as Shirley looked at her with an air of astonishment.

"Oh, yes, she was qualified to teach; you should have heard the lively discussions. I recall the interest she evoked and other traits of good teaching that I've observed now that I am older. However, it was not that that makes her my ideal teacher. The companionship and the friendship given us endeared her to us all. We all respected her dignity. Our lessons of good nature, fair play and sympathy were worth-while. She is the happiest memory I have of all my teachers. Such memories act as a steering wheel in your life if you get in deep water." Shirley paused and continued thoughtfully, "I'm not tall but that is the only way I resemble her. You are tall but you resemble her in other ways, as I told you a while ago." At that, Shirley rose and with a merry laugh rushed into the water for a swim.

"Wait for me," shouted Betty as she followed her friend into the water.

Having overheard this conversation, as I too was at the beach for the relaxation that only such a place gives one, I set to thinking about my own teaching. Did I befriend my students—the timid as well as the more forward ones? Did I make character training as important as academic? Did I neglect to teach the lessons that we can teach unconsciously? Did I cultivate a voice and a dignity that were pleasing to my personality? These thoughts rushed through my mind. Ever since retiring because of illness, I have retained my interest in my ex-students. When one proves to be a poor citizen and the law has to take care of him, I breathe a prayer for his pardon if I am the one who failed to do my duty to him. How I glow with pride if one of them is successful! I then feel that I might have helped him in my little way—especially if one tells me that I did. That does happen sometimes. I had a letter that did just that from a boy who was in military service in Europe. Such things are what make teaching worthwhile. Like a mother, a teacher often fails to get expressions of appreciation for many things that she does, until many years pass—sometimes, never.

A Hero Without a Uniform

"Well, let's talk shop. It's not time for club yet. The boys will not be here for some time yet," said Alfred Swan, the oldest of the four youths of high school age in the lounge of the local Y.M.C.A. of a small city in the Chicago vicinity.

"What's on your young and immature mind?" inquired Carter Manns, a plump, dark-eyed youth of seventeen years." What can we *undergraduates do for you?*" he added.

"A lot," answered Alfred gloomily. "It's like this. By virtue of my office as class chairman, in the absence of Miss Enson to-morrow I will be expected to give 'a bit of guidance and to stimulate the discussion'—so she says—in the discussion hour. Wow! wow! I never tried 'to guide and stimulate'! How to do it!—I don't know! And *that subject!* That's my predicament," groaned Alfred.

"Who ever heard of such a topic? Why waste precious time on it! Why not talk about something to eat, or something to see and hear at least?" questioned John, a youth of nineteen, his blue eyes sparkling like a dewy bluebell on a spring morning. At this he scrambled to his feet to offer his chair near Alfred to Professor Iller as he entered the lounge. The other boys arose politely to greet the tall, handsome young man.

"Good evening, boys," said the professor, smiling. After a

cordial greeting and the usual pleasantries were exchanged, he inquired gravely, "Why so serious?"

The boys exchanged glances and looked at Alfred. "This postgraduate wants some help and is asking us Juniors to be kind enough to help him prepare for the social science discussion for tomorrow. As Junior Class Sponsor, what do you say?" asked James McKan, a dark-haired boy of seventeen whose black eyes flashed an understanding gleam to the teacher.

"Help him of course, James," responded the professor, his handsome boyish face showing that his association with the boys as their Hi-Y sponsor was a pleasure as well as a duty.

Turning his face to Alfred he asked, "What is your topic? As I came in, I heard John's remark about it."

"That's what we are wondering. All this time you have failed to give us an idea of what you are talking about. Come! Out with it. Is it 'Oil Monopoly'?" asked Carter in a taunting tone, knowing that Alfred's father was a stockholder in a large oil company.

"No," interrupted John, his eyes giving a glance of friendly understanding to the young professor, who seemed to be a real friend to the boys, not their teacher to whom they feared to tell their secrets, "it's '*isms*.' Can you imagine a teacher choosing such a topic for *high school kids* to talk about? Who knows what to do with those troublesome things? I, for one, know nothing about them, and more, I care nothing about them," he added, as if that would dismiss the subject.

"Who in the world has been writing about isms in the *Weekly Review,* or do you Seniors use another current-events paper?" asked James. "We like the *Weekly Review* that Mr. Iller orders for us better than the one we used last year," he added, giving Mr. Iller an approving look.

"We Seniors read more than one paper," laughed John. "Miss Enson orders a number of different ones and we read whichever we please."

"You don't have us beat any there; we get three good papers in our class, don't we?" retorted Carter, turning to the professor. "But give Mr. Iller a chance to say a word; maybe he can tell us something that will *help* Alfred before we go into the Hi-Y meeting. The other boys are not all here yet."

"That's a boy! Hear our president talk, will you?" said John, looking at Alfred.

"Thank you, Carter, for giving me a chance to get an opinion that I value on this matter," responded Alfred. "But what were you about to say, Mr. Iller, when you were so rudely interrupted by our jabber?" he asked, turning his face towards the sponsor, who did look a bit bored.

"Your topic is, indeed, one that is puzzling many of us. We are all baffled, to put it mildly. It must have been the article on communism by Edward Hunter entitled 'The Lion's Mouth' that suggested this topic to Miss Enson." He paused thoughtfully for a moment and then continued: "Did I hear John say he did not care about these troublesome things? It would be too bad if everybody would say that, John."

"Well, there are fascism, communism, atheism, capitalism, idealism, Judaism, and baptism! Yes, a hundred and one more isms. Which one does she expect us to talk about?" drawled John with his usual dry humor.

"That will depend upon your chairman," said Mr. Iller. "He will choose the ism from the extensive list that you have in mind; or he may have a more inclusive one," he added, looking at Alfred.

"That is just it," interrupted Alfred. "I have no plans. I'm at a loss. I don't know what to do. Why did Miss Enson ask me to take charge of the discussion hour when she knows I never had training of that kind?" continued Alfred, asking the last question more of himself than of his companions.

"One of the chief objectives of social studies is to get us into the habit of reading, thinking, conversing, or discussing as you say it. We read too much without thinking over the things that are said to us in what we read, Alfred. Miss Enson must know you are capable of handling the situation. Plan something to say; make it interesting to the class; and use good English. As a result, all will be well," explained Mr. Iller.

"If the procedure is what bothers you, I can help you some, Alfred," volunteered John.

"It is unfortunate that one can go through high school and

never be called upon to take charge of a group. The little school that I attended before I came here had no such opportunities to give us, Mr. Iller. I hope you do not think me an infant," Alfred apologized.

"Forget it. But get your topic in mind. I know now why Miss Enson planned this for you," said Mr. Iller quietly. "She knows," he continued in a friendly voice, "that you should learn to do such things, and the only way to learn is to do. Now here is your chance. John has been in this high school long enough to be of assistance to you. He had a list of isms for you to which I might add a few. Often anti-ism groups baffle us by their misuse of our English words. They misrepresent facts by a lack of rhetorical training. More than baffling, they are actually dangerous to our nation. Groups in Washington, D.C., may be definitely opposed to communism, fascism, alcoholism, etc., but how do we know if we cannot understand their language when they make their speeches? They may be attacking individualism, republicanism, Judaism, etc. Or they may be just getting into the habit of forming abstract nouns by adding three letters to proper names. What is the meaning of all these isms? Do we know, or are we, as individuals, neglecting the most important ism of all—purism, the rigid observance of purity in the use of words? Shall we demand that leaders stop 'butchering the king's English'? What do you say, Alfred? If you present your chosen ism to the class tomorrow in simple, clear, and concise English, you will have some of these anti-ism leaders beat. Can we count on you as good citizens to be leaders in a Purism group, boys?"

The boys, knowing that Mr. Iller's ardent hobby was good English, answered unanimously, "OK"!

Laughingly he arose from his chair, saying, "Your slang will be good English some day." He turned to Alfred. "Will the questions I suggested and John's suggestions aid you in your new venture, Alfred?" he inquired.

"Oh, yes; thank you very much," responded Alfred gratefully.

"It is seven-thirty. We must go inside to our Hi-Y meeting," Mr. Iller interrupted, looking at his watch. "What have you planned for *me* this evening, Carter? Never since you were elected president of our club have we had a meeting without a definite program. Watch Carter's procedure, Alfred—he is a good chairman. You can get some helpful ideas," continued Mr. Iller as he walked beside Alfred.

"Thanks, do you want a quarter, Mr. Iller?" laughed Carter as they proceeded into the clubroom, where many principles of Christian citizenship were taught by the zealous young sponsor.

This conversation illustrates the relation of an ideal teacher, such as Shirley has in mind, and his or her students. Several years ago as I was entering the school building one morning the first week of a new semester, the Superintendent of Schools overtook me. Greeting me as usual, he then asked, "Did you see the sheik?"

"What sheik?" I countered.

"Our new history teacher of course," said he.

"I saw some new men around the building, but Mr. Smith was at Indiana University when I was there. He was at the school cafeteria yesterday. Do you refer to him?" I asked.

"No, no! I mean the one in room three-fifteen. He comes very highly recommended from Chicago University. You watch for him," he concluded as we came to the door of my room.

I soon did get acquainted with the tall, dark, handsome man in room 315. I found him not what I term a sheik but a hero without a uniform. He told me in regretful tones that he had volunteered for military service. But they told him that he would make a better teacher than a soldier. Later he told me that since childhood he had suffered a strange heart ailment from the effects of scarlet fever. He felt the disappointment but turned to his teaching wholeheartedly. All the years that we taught in the same building I observed his enthusiastic concern for the welfare of his students. He has been a successful teacher and devoted his life living for his country while many of our heroes in uniform died for it in these wars.

George Matthew Adams, in his column "Friendly Talk," said:

"The teacher experiences little or no glamor. His, or hers, is to do a job, and to put heart as well as head into the work at hand. They get no medals, and rarely any acclaim, yet they are invariably faithful, conscientious and selfless. And their work compensation is all too small."

Some Notes From a Classroom Teacher's Daily Planbook

Not long ago I met one of my friends who had retired because of her husband's disability. She told me she had been called to do some substitute work. "I never substituted at any time that was as easy to take up the work as last week," she said.

"Why was that?" I inquired.

"You know Mr. George Iller? He was injured one evening while helping some boys get ready for a program to be held at the school auditorium this Saturday. He is in the hospital now. Do you know he had the whole two weeks' daily plans written out? He must do so regularly. It was such a relief to know what to do when I went into the room!" she exclaimed.

"I have always found it advisable to have my daily plans written up for my own use. Sometimes when I did fail to do so, I was confused. That is one thing to be learned when one starts teaching. It is not too easy. Do you remember? We had one principal who came into our room and inspected our daily plans once or twice in each semester. Some of the teachers were too neglectful to please him," I concluded our conversation.

As I know how difficult it is to make lesson plans for the daily work, I am going to tell you of some ways we have done them. Different subjects demand ways of their own. You can buy blank daily planbooks for the subject you are teaching. But do beginning teachers have money to buy all the things they need? I didn't. So, necessity is the mother of invention. I found this way out of my difficulty. Following are some suggestions of my own which may be helpful:

1. I would outline the text I had to teach.
2. I then divided the subject matter into parts that we could handle.
3. Daily plans (tentative) for a month at a time, as time demands changes, can be made for an inexperienced teacher without fail.
4. There are always three elements to consider: the subject matter, time, and methods of presentation as well as the consideration of your students.

Here is one of the early plans I used when a beginning teacher in a one-room school. The ages of my students were twelve to thirteen years, combining the sixth and seventh grades. The subject matter was Longfellow's poem "Excelsior." The time was limited. The plans for its presentation were as follows:

TEACHER'S AIM	PUPIL'S AIM
To teach enjoyment of this great poem and appreciation of its moral idea.	To learn what became of the young man who attempted to climb the Alps, and to apply the incident to our own life.
Subject matter.	Method of presentation.
Simple narrative taken literally.	Describe the lofty mountain in the poet's words.
Leading facts in the literal story.	What are some dangers one meets in climbing such a lofty mountain? How do the monks come to the aid of mountain climbers? Read the poem stanza by stanza.

Meaning of difficult words and phrases.

What is meant by "device," "falchion," "clarion," "spectral," "glacier," and "startled air"?

Read the poem through carefully the second time. Now describe the region. Tell the story.

Was the young man sad or joyous? Read your answer in the words of the poet. (Verses 2, 3 and 5.)

Interpretation.

Was he attractive or unattractive in his appearance? (Verses 2, 5 and 9.)

What things tempted him to abandon his journey? (Verses 3, 4, 5 and 9.)

Do you see any good reason why he should not have stopped?

Was he then a foolish fellow or a rash adventurer?

Longfellow calls the young man beautiful, and in the last two lines suggests his ascent to heaven.

What is Longfellow's opinion of him in the last stanza?

How do you explain such approval?

Narrative taken figuratively.

Since the story is not to be taken literally, let us see how it should be interpreted.

The mountain signifies a steep road, the route necessary for an unselfish life. The happy homes and the three persons

What does the mountain signify? The happy homes? The maiden? The peasant?

signify the types of tempta-
tions or overcautious advisers.

Why is the device spoken of
as strange? . . . the tongue as
unknown? What is the meaning of "excelsior"?

Describe in full the kind of
person the poet seems to
admire.

Have you known such a
person?

The striking qualities of the
young man are unselfishness,
courage, determination and
energy.

What about Washington? . . .
Lincoln? . . . other persons
you have heard of in our history? . . . at the present time?

All efficient persons with high
ideals must show these qualities.

Do you think it is necessary
for every good person to ex-
ercise these qualities? What
is a proof of this? At what
times do we need to recall
this fact? What are the ad-
vantages of possessing a high
ideal? How is it helpful to
have a motto?

Style: diction, beauty and
force.

Find some happily chosen
words. Which stanza shows
the character of the youth
most forcibly, in your opinion? Which seems to you
most attractive?

Good oral reading.

What precautions, if any,
would you suggest for the
proper reading of the poem.
Read it aloud.

Now for some plans for social studies. "I don't care for history.
It is only a lot of names and dates. It is always about wars and

ancient things." This lament among students was often heard in the past. So our social studies were adjusted to the study of things of the past as they explain what is going on about us now. These things are not only wars and political events but ways of communication, employment, etc. Things in peacetime affect us as much as in wartime; so in our seventh-grade classes we studied United States as a nation of emigrants. We noted its development from the little new country to the wealthiest of the world. This study was followed by a comparative study of the changing people and countries of the world. We hoped thus to instill a pride in our country not only for its wealth, but in its ideas of toleration for all races and religions.

The goal of our studies was to teach the meaning of democracy, dignity of the individual, and conduct, thus to make good citizens. The following plans for a semester's work may prove helpful to you. In writing these plans I used not just one textbook but several. (At this time there was a critical study of the adopted text.) We tried to give other authors' views. We followed the unit plan of study. Our social study department agreed that there was some measure of success. The plans for my seventh grade were determined by the work of the eighth and ninth grade to insure continuity of the work of our department. It was such as indicated below:

THE SEMESTER THEME

HOW THE UNITED STATES BECAME A WORLD POWER

5 *Periods:* Unit One
How Environments Contribute to the Strength of the United States

5 *Periods:* Unit Two
New Ways of Doing Our Work

2 *Periods:* Unit Three
Developing, Using and Conserving Our National Resources

2 Periods: Unit Four
 How the United States Became an Industrial Nation

6 Periods: Unit Five
 The United States Has a Great Share in World Trade

4 Periods: Unit Six
 The United States Faces the Future

Plans for unit 1 only are given in hopes that they may aid you to get started in time making of your own plans if you have never taught:

SUBJECT MATTER	TEACHER'S ACTIVITY
Exploratory work:	Conversation in an informal way:

I. Early Civilization.
    1. Six great needs
      of man
    2. Resources
	1. To ascertain the extent of the class's former study

II. Our Own Civilization.
    1. Changing
    2. Two kinds
      a) Agricultural
      b) Industrial
	2. To lead to questions by students as aid to teacher in further work

III. Our Standard of Living.
    1. Location of home
    2. Size of family
    3. Resources
	3 To interest the students; to lead them to creative thinking and research (associated with Unit 1)

References:
    Rugg textbook I—
    Chapters I, II
    Flat pictures
    Films or slides to give some reasons for the growth of civilization
	Teacher helps to locate geographical divisions by use of a large map upon inquiries from individuals.

IV. Geography of the United States.

Map Study:

Make a Tabulation—

1. States without seacoast
2. States that touch the Great Lakes
3. States that touch the Mississippi River
4. States that touch Mexico
5. States that touch Canada

Regional locations—

1. Highlands
2. Central Plains
3. Great Western Plains, etc.

Geography references:

Pupils have to do such reading as follows—

1. In Rugg textbook I— Chapters I, II, III, IV and V
2. See books on the shelves as listed, wth pages indicated:

Principles of Human Geography, by Huntington; *Human Geography,* by Russell Smith; *Exploring Geography,* by Casner & Peatie

Teacher places some guide questions on blackboard, or gives mimeographed copies to each student for research.

These questions may be used as a basis of class discussion.

The work as planned was divided into five periods for our classwork. You cannot decide this until you know how much time you have for the work.

General science was the most difficult subject for me to plan for teaching. You may be able to do better by looking these over. We used the unit method, as most textbook writers suggest. The pages of my planbook looked something like this:

SUBJECT MATTER	PUPIL'S ACTIVITY	TEACHER'S ACTIVITY
Introduction to subject. Unit I: How scientists make discoveries. Kinds of problems: 1. Health 2. Social 3. Recreation 4. Science of the home Steps on scientific thinking: 1. Find a problem. 2. Get all known facts. 3. Make a solution of own (guess). 4. Test it (experiment). 5. State the results of your experiment.	All students given a chance to take part in the introductory talk. Study pictures on the bulletin board. Read in text as assigned. Prepare a list of questions that you must answer alone; another list that one with more experience must answer for you or help you answer. Read stories of some science heroes from books on the shelves at home. Observations: Sit outdoors where nobody will disturb you; make a list of the sounds you hear; the things you see near you; the things that are far away from you. How long did you sit and observe? Report to class.	Simple introductory talk giving primary purpose of course. 1. To understand our surroundings. 2. To learn good habits. 3. To learn to observe accurately. 4. To learn to be open-minded. 5. To find things about us that are interesting. 6. To learn how these ordinary things have always contributed to our welfare as scientists have studied them. Urge the students to do observations for classroom talk. They love this. Lead the discussion by class to show how the science heroes did scientific thinking to make their discoveries in each case.

Science is just an effort to satisfy the curiosity of the individual. The primary purpose of a science teacher is to instill this urge in the students. Student experiments at home or in the classroom (laboratory) provide student activities that give first-hand experiences. Many pages of history are written about Napoleon Bonaparte. How many of the students in our seventh grade have heard of Faraday, Galileo, Copernicus or some other scientists that have done so much for us?

What child is not interested in such questions as:

1. What causes the colors in the rainbow?
2. Why do we see lightning before we hear the thunder?
3. What holds an airplane up?
4. Why do ships float?
5. Why do apples grow on one tree, while on another tree beside it are cherries?

After reading some of the stories of the science heroes, as the assignment directed, one girl came to class with the following facts that had been of interest to her:

Luther Burbank was born in Lancaster, Massachusetts. The boy loved plants. He placed his ear to nature's heart and to him were revealed many secrets. He picked a seed-ball from his mother's potato patch. He perfected a freak plant that bore potatoes underground and tomatoes on the plant above the ground. He went to Santa Rosa, California, when he was twenty-two years of age. He perfected a strawberry plant that bears fruits the year round. He also developed many other plants such as: the spineless opuntia for cattle to feed upon in desert lands, apples of various kinds, the climax-plum, a giant stoneless prune; and lots of flowers found in our gardens.

If you have some good science hero stories, you will be surprised at the interest the students have in them.

Here is an idea from a little fourth-grade teacher that is worth thinking over before going into your classroom, no matter what subject or grade of work you are to teach*

> When I consider that parents are entrusting their children to me for six hours a day, I realize that my preparation must include more than lesson plans. I read Paul's first letter to the Corinthians (Chapter 13) and the twelfth chapter of Romans. Then I pray: "Make me a kindly and understanding teacher. Make me a friendly and patient teacher. Give me a real love for each and every one of my children, and fit me to be loved and imitated by them. Give me the strength to meet the challenge I see in their eyes."

* Reprinted through the courtesy of the author, Vera Johnson, Columbia Falls, Montana.

SOME TEACHING AIDS

During my teaching years, I learned many things the hard way. Experience is the best teacher, however. In relating some of my experiences, I hope I may help some beginning teachers. I made a study of teaching aids. This was suggested by the demand in our building by teachers who were failing to use such things as were available to them. Some of us wish for things beyond our reach and fail to see the commonplace things about us that are useful. Do we wish for things that we do not need? Have you ever visited a one-room school where the teacher had very few aids and found the students busy and happy? Why ask that? There are so few one-room schools today. That is the kind of school in which I started teaching. We had to use commonplace things. Commercial things have crowded them out. Grains of corn are displaced by colored counters for the little ones. Commercial stencils are used instead of autumn leaves, etc. We should not forget the cost when we ask for aids. Be sure the aids are not simply busy-work! When circumstance calls for an aid, then is the time to use aids. A purposeless use of them is a waste of time and energy. With a purpose, find an aid.

What boy is not happy making an airplane model in a study unit in general science, or in a social science study in transportation? If he finds his own material, so much the better. If other children help supply his needs, they learn lessons of co-operation too. Among teaching aids none excel visual aids. "One look is better than a thousand words," is an old Chinese adage which we find true.

VISUAL AIDS

Commercial education of the public is by visual aids. Visual education is really a teaching process. It consists of selecting, organizing and using various tools and devices. Look at the road signs! Posters, cartoons or other devices get the ideas across to the public. They educate the memory, the intellect, and the critical faculties. Thus, language symbols can even be interpreted by children. Among the aids we used in our classes, the following are most readily recalled:

1. Construction work
2. Demonstrations; radio programs
3. Visual aids
   a) Blackboard
   b) Bulletin board
   c) Cartoons
   d) Charts
   e) Diagrams
   f) Exhibits
   g) Drawings
   h) Flash-cards
   i) Globes
   j) Maps
   k) Models
   l) Slides
   m) Silent films
   n) Sound films
   o) Stereographs

With T.V. coming to the schools, it seems to me that lots of good can be derived from it. When the radio and T.V. are well adjusted to the service of teachers, much good is due. They will soon be adjusted, we trust. How to use a classroom film is important. All these aids are only effective when used with a purpose in mind. The department of audio-visual aids prepared some instruction for us which I will pass on to you.

HOW TO USE CLASSROOM FILMS (SOUND OR SILENT)

The following procedure has grown out of investigations in the classroom use of films during the past several years. It is not represented as the one and only method of film utilization, but one which has been found highly effective when used in a variety of situations.

1. Before the film is shown, the teacher should be sure that purposes for its study are established in the minds of all the students. The purposes may well be stated on the blackboard or written in the students' notebooks. In each case the teacher should be well acquainted with the content of the film (having studied it herself). An accompanying handbook will reveal to her the number and type of ideas clarified by the film. This will permit plans to be made for association of them to the interests and needs of the students.

2. Present the films.

3. Immediately after the showing, during the same class period, if possible, initiate a discussion of the three things accomplished.

   a) Ascertain the extent to which the study class has achieved the purposes for which the film was shown.

   b) This discussion will lead to many questions and comments by the pupils which should be noted by the teacher and used in setting up purposes for additional showings of the films.

   c) Use the interest aroused by the film as a springboard into the broader study of the unit. This will lead into many types of research and creative thinking; oral and written language; art; dramatics; and other activities associated with the study of the unit.

Frank Glenn, a well-known educator, once said, "I am sure we could reduce time, cost and raise the quality and appeal of education if we set our minds through the study of how to teach by means of the eye more."

Control of Classroom Activities

"Dear Shirley: I'm still taking life easy down here in Arizona. Your letter was a pleasant surprise to me. I did not know you were teaching in that building. That is where I spent many years. Do you remember? I am sorry that you are a little disappointed with the work. Most of us are at first. There are so many perplexing problems to face. Do not hope 'to do everything that will please everybody.' Jesus did not please all, so how can we expect to do so? Do your best and that is all one can do. I will try to answer some of your questions, but do not take what I say to be infallible.

"You ask me how to get control of the group activities; and how to get the group to working without having the disturbing things occurring so often. Well, that is an old, old problem. I will tell you some things that you already know but have failed to think of:

1. First, do not expect too much of yourself or your students.
2. Remember your own student days. Be true to yourself and make friends of your students.
3. Be firm in all your demands but be *sure* you do not ask somebody to do something that it is not possible for him to do. Some cannot do certain things as well as others can. For example, I cannot sing like you can sing.

"Control of the activities in our schoolroom is one of the most perplexing of a teacher's numerous problems. Youngsters may be even more mischievous than they were years ago, but they must be more clever too. The lack of the famous "big geography" that you never used but that some of the balding fathers will remember makes detecting the extracurricular activities (shall we call them this?) such as writing notes, reading funny papers, etc., more easily accomplished. Just be your very self as I remember you, and you will make good friends of your pupils.

"One of my late principals was a help in our teaching. I hope you will have one as a support to you in the beginning of your teaching career. One year he handed us a bulletin on our evaluation for the year. In it he quoted from some materials furnished him at a principals' conference that he had attended. The material below is a part of the bulletin. Maybe it will help you as it did me at the time. The following part was under the title 'Control Technics':

1. Keep all students busy. Have them doing something useful.
2. Make the students like you. Be the kind of a person they want to please instead of tease.
3. Give each child work that he can do. The course must be adjusted to the class, not the class to the course.
4. Don't delay punishment. Have it over as soon as possible and make a new start.
5. Don't threaten. Threats usually serve only to fan the smoldering embers of resentment.
6. Don't leave children unsupervised. Usually this practice cannot be justified.
7. Don't fail to turn a case over to the principal if you cannot handle it yourself.
8. Don't expect your principal to work wonders with a shingle. Years, not minutes, are required to change the problem child into a good citizen.
9. Give encouragement when a child does something well. (This too often is forgotten.) This is a common fault of many people in our everyday life. We forget to commend but we do condemn.

10. Work with the students in your class as a coach works with his team. You are not a taskmaster. The children should be working for themselves, not for the teacher.
11. Be fair. When a child is treated unfairly by an adult who is in a position of responsibility, the damage is almost incalculable. If we expect children to be fair with us, how much more will they expect us to be fair with them.
12. Be courteous. Being discourteous to children has the same effect on them as their discourtesy has upon us.
13. Be firm. Strength and power are among the things that children admire.
14. Keep yourself strong. Learn how to sleep soundly at night, and how to use your week-ends and vacations for recreation and relaxation. Such a person will not be annoyed easily.
15. Be enthusiastic about things you do at school. The teacher with the sparkle of enthusiasm about his work finds that his classes, too, are enthusiastic.

"The following little poem contains some questions which we should ask ourselves when we realize how our lives influence others:

As I Go My Way

My life may touch a million lives in some way
    ere I go from this old world of struggle to a
    place I do not know,
So this I wish I always wish, the prayer I always pray,
Let my life help the other lives it touches by the way.

"I do not know who wrote the poem, but it expresses the thoughts I wish to leave with you.
"I am your sincere friend,

                                 Miss Finley"

WHY TEACH?

A Teacher's Mistake

When a statistician makes a mistake, nobody knows but he;
And when a lawyer loses his case, he promptly raises his fee.
Should a legislator skid, it becomes a law profound;
If a physician slips, they bury it six feet underground;
But when a teacher makes a mistake . . . WOW!
Mamas and papas, uncles and aunts, jump on her and HOW!

Editors editorialize;
Social workers moralize;
And nobody dares to sympathize.
Taxpayers howl in honest wrath;
The humblest doggie avoids her path.
She is loudly condemned by the PTA; NYA; PWA;
And what is left of the WPA.
She is promptly told where to go and HOW;
When a teacher makes a mistake . . . WOW!*

Do you know a teacher who has been decorated for valor or
received some outstanding honor for service? Oh, yes, there are

* Reprinted from the Delaware *School Journal.*

many teachers in the armed forces and auxiliaries that have, but how many for superb services in teaching? Which is better—to prepare others for the difficulties of adult life, or to die for the mistakes of our generation? Every classroom is a citadel of democracy if the teaching is worth-while. Why do many teachers return to teaching after trying other jobs?

Miss Hilblink, of the Nebraska public schools, tells us her experience. This is much like the experiences of others to whom I have talked. In part, Miss Hilblink said: "I left my teaching and went in the spring to Washington, D.C. As I stepped from the train at Union Station and walked through the depot, where we see more tired people than any other place, I beheld the Capitol building, the dome shining like a jewel. I thought, 'Here is the place . . . the heart of the nation . . . where I can really do something.' When I closed my books and locked my classroom back home, I felt that I was leaving a job of minor importance.

"It took four months of hard work for Uncle Sam to make me realize the situation. As September drew near, letters came to me telling of the need for teachers. The Nebraska newspapers reached me, commenting on the great need. I was disturbed. I had reasonably responsible duties to do at the office, but I knew we must have teachers to have a satisfactory world. Every time I looked about me in Washington, I could see the pages of history unfold. I could see men like George Washington, Abraham Lincoln and scores of others sweating and toiling to create this nation. I could see the value of human character in the up-building of our country. As a teacher I had a part in the formation of that character. As an office worker, I was a cog in a machine.

"Every time I thought of my locked classroom, I knew that I had locked my heart behind those doors. Every time I stepped into the Library of Congress or the Smithsonian Institute, I saw something that reminded me of my unfinished task in the school. I was learning every month that my higher salary was being spent to meet a higher cost of living. I was doing a job another person could do at no increase in my savings and at a loss in personal satisfaction. My place in Washington could be filled; my place in the Nebraska school was still open. I resigned my post. The decision gave me immense relief. I am now back in school." Thus she ends the story happily. Our friend Miss Hilblink is only one of many who tell us such experiences.

"Why sign a contract for another year," said Miss Temp to herself at the end of the school day in late September. This she told us during a siege of shoptalk to which teachers are accustomed. I've heard a bank teller say, "I am not going to eat at the table with that bunch of teachers. All they talk about is school."

I am sorry to say this is often true. Well, on with our shoptalk. "Maybe I've taught too long," Miss Temp continued. "No, twenty years is not too long, I thought, when it makes one happy. My gaze wandered up and down the rows of desks, and I thought of the children who sat in each one. The sunlight fell upon a picture on the wall. In the background was a group of wounded soldiers limping home with defeat upon their faces. In the foreground was a young face radiating so much strength and courage that you failed to notice the crutch he was carrying. Years ago when I hung that picture, some of the teachers said, 'Why do you want that dreary picture in front of you all day?' It did look dreary to me now, so I got up and took it down. I put it in the desk drawer. Because I felt . . . just how did I feel?—that I was not needed here. I thought I would not sign my contract and go to some other kind of work. I looked at my watch. Charles, the boy that I had given an extra hour each week, was late again as usual.

"'Gosh, I'm late. I've been cramming . . . I hope I make this test,' said Charles as he came rushing into the room with no bit of apology.

"'Here it is,' I said as I handed him a sheet of questions.

"There was just the sound of the scratching of Charles' pen for some time. 'Gee, you took the picture down, didn't you?' he said suddenly. 'You know, I sort of went for that picture. That beat-up soldier in the front made you feel that whatever happens to you, you've got to be brave enough to keep going. . . . Well, I'm through!' said Charles, handing me his paper. 'I hope I pass.' He was gone without a word of appreciation.

"I laid my head upon the desk and sobbed. Ten minutes later I roused myself and began to grade Charles' paper, feeling somewhat better to find the paper very good . . . almost perfect, in fact. When I reached the bottom I found a note. It read as follows:

DEAR MISS TEMP:

I'm not much at talking, but I wanted you to know that I consider you my very best friend. When I came here, I was so homesick and scared that I would have died if it had not been for you. Thank you, and I hope you won't mind if I think of you like my mother, as she is dead. I shall always love you.

CHARLES CREAM

"When I read that, I suddenly did not feel tired. I took the picture out of the desk and put it back where it belonged. I then signed my contract for another year."

To my young friends who expect to teach, I will say that the experiences of these friends are similar to most of ours. If you are taking up this profession to get honor, awards and money, stop now and reconsider. There are no such awards coming your way. True, the personal satisfaction that comes sometimes comes so late that we never know what good we have done. There is the satisfaction of knowing we have done our best if we make our teaching worth-while. When my aunt, who taught for many years, passed away, Uncle told another niece and myself to divide her library between us, as we were both teachers. One day not long ago I took up one of her books which must have been borrowed at some time by one of her students. I found a short rhyme. It went as follows:

Miss Dellinger

She is a very sweet woman.
We can't tell how she is Roman;
She is full of fun
Which she shares with everyone.

Had my aunt ever seen this rhyme? Maybe not, but I do know that in her last days she did get lots of satisfaction in seeing many of her students become successful citizens. Thus she realized that her work had not been in vain.

A TEACHER'S PAY*

You look back to the misty sea of faces that were once your pupils and think of how so many of them have grown into fine young men and women, think of the ones who still write to you and visit you and ask your advice, and of the ones you meet unexpectedly on the streets, and the glad tone of their voices when they greet you. And you love them all and are very proud to have been their teacher. Then you think, "This is my pay!" And you know that regardless of the size of a teacher's check, this will always be her real pay.

* By Blanche Seale Hunt. Reprinted from the *Oklahoma Teacher*.

BEGINNING WEEK

Unless you are a person that likes to meet new friends and likes new adventures, your orientation as a new teacher is a trying ordeal. So be sure you have chosen to teach because you are convinced that you will get the satisfaction of serving that will make you useful. Too many take up teaching with the idea of awards, prestige and money. Make your choice and become professional. Dame Fortune will not tap you on the shoulder . . . and presto . . . you are a success. We get there by hard working experience. That is the hard way. But Robert Louis Stevenson said of his profession, "No other profession offers one his daily bread upon such joyful terms." This would I too say of teaching as a profession.

A spring planning of a social event by the advisory council often gives a new teacher a chance to meet her new associates. A welcome banquet is planned in some communities. These times are to be "good times." If these events are only a tea or a wiener roast, it is important for a new teacher to meet her associates halfway. Become one of the group having a good time. Later in the week you can become familiar with the school system and get ready for your classwork.

One committee had posters as a reminder to all. One poster showed a typical cartoon teacher and this rhyme:

Remember your first teaching days—
Each smile and pleasant work
Meant more than you could tell;
Let's make our welcome heard.

This short statement of current practices may give you an idea of what to expect in your first teaching week.

THE GROWING TEACHER

The leading personality in a classroom is the teacher. This is agreed. Her contribution as a person is unlimited. Of the teacher it has been said, "Her echoes roll from soul to soul." This influence extends not only to the hundreds of students but beyond them to thousands with whom they come in contact. This is a great trust. To be worthy of such a trust, one should do as an accountant who audits his books regularly—check up on one's strengths and weaknesses often. A balance sheet of the assets and liabilities in one's health, appearance, professional skills and personality will aid a growing teacher in reaching greatest usefulness. If you wish, you can make a check list of your own; this will help you find any minor defects of which you are unaware. You can ask some friend whose judgment you trust to go over the list with you. Criticism, like honest confession, is good for the soul. The ability to take criticism is a rare virtue. A teacher who is able to take it is already "a growing teacher."

Such things as health, personal appearance and professional skills are suggested for the check list. Some questions that you might list are as follows:

Health
   1.   Have I the strength that comes with good health?

2. Are my health habits sensible and regular?
3. Do I avoid the habits that are injurious?
4. Do I use my nerves as an alibi often?
5. Have I cheerfulness of spirit that bespeaks good mental and spiritual health?
6. Have I chosen a dentist and physician?

Personality
1. Do I have a sense of humor even when the joke is on me?
2. Do I speak tactfully and kindly? Am I too outspoken?
3. Can I remain calm and poised in spite of provocation and criticism, refusing to have my "feelings hurt"?
4. Do I meet people easily?
5. Am I well-informed on current events and other areas for conversation? Do I talk shop?
6. Am I constantly on the alert to improve my English? Do I seek to increase my vocabulary?

Appearance
1. Am I well-groomed?
2. Are my fingernails clean and well-kept, hair neat, clothes pressed and shoes in repair?
3. Do I stand erect or lean on desk, tables, etc.?
4. Do I avoid mannerisms?
5. Do I avoid monotony in clothes, etc.?
6. Is my carriage graceful and easy?

Professional Skills and Growth
1. Do I participate in the local, state, and national associations?
2. Do I enrich my work by professional reading, travel, summer school, etc.?
3. Do I abide by the code of ethics of the profession?
4. Am I spending some of my salary for well-chosen books?
5. Do I ever write up my classwork experiences for publication or for consideration by my fellow teachers?
6. Would I rather teach than do anything else?

The great purpose in a teacher's growth is to make a difference in the lives of others. Are your students happier, wiser, more useful and cooperative because they have known you? By this check list a teacher can measure achievements. Every teacher who looks beyond the moment will keep in touch with the students and will realize the glory and greatness of teaching. True, like anyone else, we are often disappointed with our handiwork. More often we feel a pride in the success of some of our former students—at least if one tells us of something that we did that proved of great use to them.

GOOD HABITS

Theories about what to teach and what to learn are myriad. Recently, President Day of Cornell, speaking before the Institute of Parent Leadership, gave an excellent outline of his ideas. He said that the individual has six educational needs:

1. To acquire the basic skills such as reading and writing
2. To cultivate interest or sensitivity
3. To form good work habits
4. To learn to live with one's feelings
5. To protect health and induce good health habits, especially in mental health
6. To cultivate the art of critical thinking

Those who do not acquire good work habits, health habits and emotional habits are the perpetual juveniles, the grown-up children who never seem able to do their part of the world's work, because they have never got ready for the supreme and endless duty and satisfaction of critical thinking.

Good Citizens Are Our Goal

The North Central Teachers Association of Indiana emphasized
the safeguarding of the American way of life in 1950 as a responsibility of the schools. To teach the American way of life, which is
founded upon the dignity and worth of the individual, the
youth must be taught to know it, to believe in it and to live it
continually. It behooves a teacher to be worthy of public trust;
to refrain from any affiliations which might be detrimental to the
government; to have qualities of self-discipline and a sense of
personal responsibility. This is essential for the success of our
way of life. The future teachers of America—that is, you—shall
be called to safeguard our way of life in the world struggle
between the Eastern and Western philosophies. America belongs
to the youth, and youth must be prepared for the responsibility.

The function of schools in a community is that of guiding
ethical evolution. School is life modified by the community. Some
institutions degrade, while others uplift. The church, lodges and
clubs all raise the morale of a student to the extent of their
leaders. It is from the adults that youth gets its pattern for living.
Where desirable patterns are set, we see the youth grow toward
them. Thus teacher-parent-community cooperation is an intelli-
gent way of discovering the areas of interest for the best growth
of a *wholesome, integrated individual.* The youth of today is in
need of ability to understand and combine relationships that are

new to them. Some adverse institutions are taverns, saloons, public dance halls and other places of questionable practices. The school as a discriminating factor in society dares not dictate to society. To draw the best from such a mass of patterns of behavior is a difficult task. That is what the teacher is called upon to do. Dr. Cox of Columbia University said in a class that I attended, "We must treat the students as we wish them to be, not as they are." The degree of participation by students, parents and teachers will decide the success of the school. But the personality of the teacher is probably the deciding force.

The value of understanding is recognized by the man of the street. We are told in the Bible that "understanding passeth knowledge" (Proverbs 4:7). Nobody cares too much for a walking-dictionary type of person. All realize that effective living depends upon understanding. This applies to farmers, grocers, baseball pitchers, teachers or students. Such expressions as "Do you catch on?" "Do you follow me?" or "Oh, I get you!" are evidences of the practical value of understanding. The meaning of civil liberty, democracy, the dignity of the individual and social welfare can be learned by skillful democratic actions practiced in school.

Your time in classroom is so limited that you will throw your hands up in despair when you get to the place for your activities. We all faced such tasks in the time of the World War that you have heard so much of from your elders. You, a new teacher, will be overwhelmed at the tasks you find. But do your best, your very best, and trust God for the results. In this materialistic age it is well to pause at the beginning of the day to impress upon the minds of our students the fact that our great leaders were men of great spiritual and religious types. The study of the lives of our great leaders may stimulate character development. A teacher may choose such material as time and conditions permit. Variety of presentation is most effective. The anniversaries of events and birthdays of great leaders may be beneficial though they be presented hurriedly. Blackboard messages, Bible readings, and talks are often good devices for presenting some desired lessons.

You may find some use for the following quotations. This procedure may prove worth-while:

Quotation A may remain on the front blackboard for a day; then be erased. The following morning some volunteer is asked to quote it from memory. The letter A is then written on the board with that student's name following it. The same procedure takes place the next morning with quotation B. Each time the recitation begins with A and proceeds to the latest quotation studied. The aim is to have them all memorized by the twenty-seventh day. Copying the quotations and taking them home might prove valuable to the slower students and of interest to some parents.

Other uses for these quotations may occur to you. They are as follows:

A CHARACTER ALPHABET

A good conscience is a continual Christmas.—FRANKLIN

B–e not merely good; be good for something.—THOREAU

C–haracter is much easier kept than recovered.—PAINE

D–ifficulties strengthen the mind as labor does the body.—SENECA

E–vil life is one kind of death.—OVID

F–rom errors of others a wise man corrects his own.
                                        —PUBLIUS SYRUS

G–uided by the example and good works of others, we must rely
    mainly upon our own efforts.—SAMUEL SMILES

H–e who purposely cheats his friend would cheat his God.
                                        —LAVATER

I fear nothing but doing wrong.—STERNE

J–udge thyself with a judgment of sincerity, and thou wilt judge
    others with judgment of charity.—MASON

K–nowledge, like everything else of the highest value, is not to
    be obtained easily.—ARNOLD

L–incoln's immortal character has thrown in the shade the
    splendors of his intellect.—NEWMAN

M–usic washes away from the soul the dust of everyday life.
                                        —AUERBACH

N–othing great was ever achieved without enthusiasm.—EMERSON

O–ne cannot always be a hero, but one can always be a man.

—GOETHE

P–oliteness smooths wrinkles.—JOUBERT

Q–ualities of the heart, not those of the face, should attract us.

—LAMARTINE

R–esponsibility educates.—PHILLIPS

S–unday is the golden clasp that binds together the volume of
    the week.—LONGFELLOW

T–he measure of life is not length, but honesty.—LYLY

U–nkind language is sure to produce the fruits of unkindness—
    that is, suffering in others.—BENTHAM

V–alor is like honesty; it enters into all that a man does.

—H. W. SHAW

W–e enjoy thoroughly only the pleasure that we give.—DUMAS

X–perience shows that success is due less to ability than to zeal.

—BUXTON

Y–our face is a book where men may read strange matters.

—SHAKESPEARE

Z–eal and duty are not slow.—MILTON

Some Things We Might Well Avoid

There are many problems that a teacher of the seventh grade in a junior high school of a 6–3–3 system has that other teachers do not confront. Objectives pertinent to the seventh grade are:

1. Orientation of the new students (helping them get acquainted with their new environment).
2. Observing the citizenship of the new individuals (their practice in right living).
3. Meeting the new personalities (understanding each individual in the groups).
4. Observing the scholarship of the new students (discerning the general and specific abilities and skills of each).

Orientation of the students is perhaps no more important than the teacher's understanding them.

Having met the seventh grade of our 6–3–3 system several semesters when they came to junior high from all parts of the city, I used various devices to help me avoid mistakes. One year, when I met my new classes I gave this questionnaire to some of them:

1. What are some things that you wish the teachers in junior high school would not do?

2. What do you wish teachers to do when you are in their room?
3. What do you like best to do in class time?
4. What do you dislike to do most in class time?

As I find their papers in my files yet, I will tell you about them. The reports of one class of twenty-eight were of great interest. Among their answers to question number one I found the following comments on what the teacher should avoid:

1. I wish the junior high teachers would not yell at us; at least, not yell all the time.
2. Teachers give too much homework; forget to grade our papers. (The girl who said this proved to be a good student.)
3. They sometimes hit somebody; get mad at somebody right away; get mad and scold you for something that you did not do; get in a fight with somebody and take it out on you; scold you when you have done nothing wrong; tell you "shut up" before you explain.
4. Some teachers walk up and down the room; stand by the window.
5. They do things they do not allow the students to do—chew gum; talk about their family; tell what they did when they were little.
6. They make us write everything.
7. They waste time when we are studying something interesting.
8. They keep us after the bell rings; keep us for a period after school.
9. They say someone is the lowest in the class.
10. They fail to hear your question before they start to answer it.

Others repeated some of these comments in other words: "I hope no teacher says somebody is the lowest in the class." The girl who said this proved to be an earnest worker, but she was seldom able to do the work as well as others. However, she was a good citizen, very helpful, so I was glad to get her suggestion. I am sure that she did much good in her world even if she did not carry off class honors. These are the students that appreciate a little extra attention. But do they get it? All competition should be friendly. Some folks decry all competition. We find many students like this girl. But in the adult world we meet competition. The best students should be barred from contests with the slow ones and be pitted against students of their own caliber. Thus the slow ones will not be discouraged. Some who are slow in arithmetic may be hustlers in some other subjects. By having contests in all subjects, nobody need be discouraged. Contests may be used to excess.

"Stay after school"—isn't that a familiar phrase? How many times have you heard it? Staying after school is like a quack medicine. This little verse states the case from a child's viewpoint:

> I'm "kep' in" when I'm tardy, an' I'm "kep' in" when
> I'm late;
> I'm "kep' in" for position—that means not settin' straight.
> I'm "kep' in" when my marbles comes rattlin' from
> my pockets,
> An' sometimes when my matches get mixed up with
> my rockets.
> I'm "kep' in" ef I whisper, an' I'm "kep' in" ef I chaw
> The piece of gum I've borrowed an' am warmin' in
> my jaw!
> The truth is that I'm "kep' in" for most every thing I do!
> But the jolly thing about it is the teacher's "kep' in" too!

In a teachers' journal we saw a query, "What Should Be Done With Pupils That Are Kept After School?" Well, the first thing to do is let them out. So it was decided. If Johnny cannot take care of his marbles, take care of them yourself a few days. If Susan cannot repress her giggles, let her take a book and withdraw to another room where she cannot disturb anyone. Keeping students after school is a confession of weakness, we are told. Strong teachers do not do it. Great, active, wholesome teachers bring to their classes an enthusiasm which carries the pupils along in spite of themselves. A tired teacher after school is hardly able to do a student much good when the strain of the day's work is upon her. Of course, I do not mean by this that a pupil who has been absent or is dull or defective is never to be helped after school, but that is his privilege, not a mode of punishment. Teach the student that it is a privilege to stay after school. Let him learn in schooltime and take his rebuke such as he deserves then too.

It takes tact, a quick wit and keenness to be able to be ready with a rebuke when it is deserved. One must be ever ready with an immediate and fair rebuke. Invent penalties as occasions demand them.

One boy wrote, "Teachers should not hit somebody." His simple answer told me to watch for some unpleasant experience. Later we found him to be a problem for the teachers. He was expelled for some violence. With this little hint of his, I did not have trouble with him myself. I learned of his unhappy home and sympathized with him.

The next paper was written by a boy in a nice manly handwriting. He said, "Teachers should not do things they do not allow the students to do." This boy proved to be a good citizen, and we might well heed his suggestion. The paper that followed his led me to think that the girl had had the same teacher and she was enumerating the things that he had been thinking of when he wrote his answer. She said, "Teachers should not chew gum; stand by the window; talk about their family; tell what they did when little," etc. Their suggestions were timely. "They should not waste time when we are studying something interesting." Do we waste time when we are studying something interesting; in other words, do we talk too much? An investigation by a superintendent recently showed that when ten teachers visited, they talked 80–90% of the time, while students talked only 10–20% of the time. If self-activity is necessary for the growth of the student, then the students were not growing. Real teaching is not measured by weariness of tongue muscles. The morning prayer of every teacher should be, "Help me this day to talk little and teach much; to repress my own expression and secure from my students full expression of their clear thinking and thorough understanding."

Somebody said, "I don't like teachers that tell you to shut up before you can explain; that get mad and scold; bawl you out for something you did not do; scold all the time." In these answers to the first question I found much food for thought.

Various answers to question number two followed in different words:

"I like teachers that make us happy and are pleasant; explain things when you have been absent from class and come back. I wish a teacher would not be silly but would explain things; if I get into trouble, would talk to me; let us do things that we approve."

"To make us happy and be pleasant"—concerning that task, one teacher asked, "How important is this?" When we have a hard day or something unpleasant and somebody has to be punished, I never dismiss the class without a merry song, a funny story or some joke. The students often forget the grievance and come back happy. This plea for a happy teacher is general. I do not mean that a teacher must be continually making bright conversation. Nothing destroys the poise of a class as much as a talkative teacher. She can waste time or be silly, as one student said. I spoke of the principal who was helpful to me, so I am again inserting some notes that he gave us after he had attended a principals' meeting. These notes he handed to all of his teachers:

Teacher Activity—"Talk Less and Act More"

1. Does the teacher act as the director of the class discussion?
2. Does the teacher seem to have the attitude that the discussion period belongs to the pupils?
3. Do the teacher's questions call for discussions?
4. Does the teacher insist that pupils formulate and express their own opinions?
5. Does the teacher keep the topic clearly before the class?
6. Does the teacher allow the class to divert to important discussions?
7. Does the teacher call for oral reports as a part of the discussion rather than as an isolated part of the lesson?
8. Are oral reports sufficiently few to hold interest?

9. Does the teacher resort to many methods to secure a maximum of socialization and participation?
10. Does the teacher cultivate the community atmosphere in the class?
11. Does he encourage pupils who have mastered a section of the work to help those in difficulty?
12. Does the teacher help pupils form new concepts, attitudes, or ideals instead of the memorization of a given number of facts?
13. Does the teacher seek to develop in the pupil a keener observation of the social and economic phenomena in the community?
14. Does he place emphasis on present-day conditions in social, economic and civic fields?
15. Is the lesson presented so as to make action rather than knowledge the end of learning?

The answers to question three told me some activities that my students desired. One boy, who later proved to be a good student and a good citizen, said, "I like to speak on countries; make maps; and answer questions." Twenty out of the twenty-eight answered likewise. Fifteen of the twenty-eight said they liked to read; three mentioned oral reading. Only nine of them liked to make exhibits, etc.

The answers to question four varied as the experience of the students had varied. Only two, who proved to be honor students, did not answer. Some said they did not like to read so much; write so much; follow outlines. We found that too much of one activity was the common dislike. One girl put it thus: "I do not like to do the same thing all the time."

An everlasting sameness is a bore to any alert, keen-minded student. In a letter recently received from my niece in high school, she wrote, "I get so tired of the same thing over and over." The student has a right to tire. We grant that there is much of schoolroom learning that can be mastered only by plain, unornamented drill. But the clinching power may be doubled by a decided change in tactics. "Old wine in new bottles," shall we say? In the millinery parlor, when a first creation was brought out to a lady customer recently, she said, "Thank you, that is pretty, but it is too much like my old hat. I should like a change." So with all of us.

We do not advocate a play school. But by the benefit of this little questionnaire, I'm inclined to think we should make school life as pleasant as possible. If we can vary the proceedings and get the students to be full of zest, more can be accomplished. Of course we have no right to use the time and taxpayers' money for anything that will not give direct, useful and efficient results.

CLASSROOM BONERS

TEACHER: Johnny, take that gum out of your mouth . . . and . . . put your feet in.

         ❈   ❈   ❈

TEACHER: You can't sleep in this class, James.
JAMES: I could if you did not talk so loud.

         ❈   ❈   ❈

TEACHER: What makes you late this morning, Mary?
MARY: Why, you see . . . there are eight in our family.
TEACHER: Well?
MARY: And . . . the alarm was set for only seven.

         ❈   ❈   ❈

SCIENCE TEACHER: Name a liquid that won't freeze, Robert.
ROBERT: Hot water.

         ❈   ❈   ❈

TEACHER: Now, children, I want you to be so very still you can hear a pin drop.
LITTLE WILLIE (after a silence):   "O.K., teacher, let 'er drop.

         ❈   ❈   ❈

TEACHER: Susan, what is one-fiftieth of three-sixteenths?
SUSAN: I don't know exactly but it isn't enough to worry about.

TEACHER: Is there a word in the English language that contains all the vowels?

ENGLISH STUDENT: Unquestionably.

TEACHER: What is it?

ENGLISH STUDENT: I told you.

*   *   *

TEACHER: This is the fifth time this week that I've had to punish you. What do you say?

LITTLE BOBBIE: I'm glad it's Friday.

A Prayer for Teachers*

O God, Thou who hast ever brought all life to its perfection by patient growth, grant me patience to guide my pupils to the best in life.

Teach me to use the compulsion of love and of interest; and save me from the weakness of coercion.

Make me one who is a vitalizer of life and not a merchant of facts.

Show me how to overcome the forces that destroy by harnessing the urges that lead to the life abundant.

Give me such a sense of value that I may distinguish the things that last from those that pass, and never confuse mountains with molehills.

Grant me insight to overlook the faults of exuberance because I can see with prophetic eye the possibilities of enthusiasm.

Save me, O Lord, from confusing that which is evil with that which is only immature.

May I learn the laws of human life so well that, saved from the folly of reward and punishment, I may help each pupil of mine to find a supreme devotion for which he will give his all. And may that devotion be in tune with Thy purpose for Thy world.

* By Chaplain Wallace Grant Fiske, O.C.S., AAFETTI. Reprinted through the courtesy of the National Education Association *Journal*.

May I be so humble and keep so young that I may continue to grow and to learn while I teach.

Grant that I may strive not so much to be called a teacher as to be a teacher; not so much to speak of Thee, but to reveal Thee; not so much to talk about love and human service, but to be the spirit of these; not so much to speak of the ideals of Jesus, but in every act of my teaching to reveal His ideals.

Save me from letting my work become commonplace by the ever-present thought that, of all human endeavors, teaching is most like the work that Thou hast been doing through all the generations. Amen.